LIFEWAYS

The Powhatan

RAYMOND BIAL

BENCHMARK BOOKS

MARSHALL CAVENDISH
NEW YORK

SERIES CONSULTANT: JOHN BIERHORST

ACKNOWLEDGMENTS

This book would not have been possible without the kind help of several individuals and organizations who have devoted themselves to preserving the culture of the Powhatan. I would like to especially thank Tracy Blevins and the staff at the Jamestown Settlement for their assistance and permission to photograph at the Powhatan village there. I would also like to acknowledge Debora Moore and her mother Gentle Rain for permission to photograph at the Pamunkey Indian Museum, as well as River-Man and Redwing who operate the River Side Pottery Shop on the Mattaponi Indian Reservation. I would also like to acknowledge the kind assistance of the National Archives and the Library of Congress for providing a number of historical illustrations.

I am again indebted to Kate Nunn and Doug Sanders for guiding this project from concept to finished book and to John Bierhorst for his thorough review of the manuscript and help in locating appropriate stories. I would like to gratefully acknowledge my wife, Linda, and my children Anna, Sarah, and Luke, especially for their help during our trip to the coastal plain of Virginia to make photographs for this book.

This book is respectfully dedicated to the Powhatan who are working to keep alive the spirit of their ancestors.

Contents

Author's Note

At the dawn of the twentieth century, Native Americans were thought to be a vanishing race. However, despite four hundred years of warfare, deprivation, and disease, American Indians have not gone away. Countless thousands have lost their lives, but over the course of this century the populations of native tribes have grown tremendously. Even as American Indians struggle to adapt to modern Western life, they have also kept the flame of their traditions alive—the language, religion, stories, and the everyday ways of life. An exhilarating renaissance in Native American culture is now sweeping the nation from coast to coast.

The Lifeways books depict the social and cultural life of the major nations, from the early history of native peoples in North America to their present-day struggles for survival and dignity. Historical and contemporary photographs of traditional subjects, as well as period illustrations, are blended throughout each book so that readers may gain a sense of family life in a tipi, a hogan, or a longhouse.

No single book can comprehensively portray the intricate and varied lifeways of an entire tribe, or nation. I only hope that young people will come away with a deeper appreciation for the rich tapestry of Indian culture—both then and now—and a keen desire to learn more about these first Americans.

1. Origins

For centuries,
the Powhatan lived along
the coast of the Atlantic Ocean
in what is now the state of
Virginia.

WHEN EVERYONE HAD SETTLED INTO THEIR LODGES AT NIGHT AND GATHERED around the flickering light of the fire, the elders told stories. The following retelling is based on a story from the Patawomeck, a small tribe that belonged to the Powhatan Confederacy. With from 160 to 200 warriors, the Patawomeck, whose name may mean "trading place," lived in Virginia in the 1600s.

The Creation Story

There were five gods. The chief god assumed the form of Great Hare. The other gods were the winds, invisible and without shape, flowing from the corners of the earth.

One day, Great Hare decided that he would create people and animals to live on the earth. He made various kinds of women and men, but he tied them up in a large bag. Powerful giants, who were cannibal spirits, came to Great Hare's dwelling place in the east, toward the rising sun. The giants wanted to eat the people, but Great Hare scolded them and drove them away.

Great Hare then made the rivers and lakes, as well as the vast ocean and all the fish that swim there. He created the forests and meadows and the deer that lived there, nibbling on leaves and grass.

Jealous of Great Hare and his work, the wind gods gathered from the four directions. With hunting poles, they killed the deer and held a grand feast. Afterward, they returned to the east, west, north, and south.

Having observed the malicious deed of the wind gods, the Great Hare picked up all the hairs of the slain deer and scattered them over

Footpaths that led to other villages and hunting grounds crisscrossed the dense, shadowy forests of Powhatan territory.

the earth. As he did, he spoke sacred words and cast powerful spells. Each hair became a deer. He then opened the bag and placed the women and men upon the earth. Each pair had children, and the earth came to be peopled.

POWHATAN WAS THE NAME OF BOTH AN INDIVIDUAL TRIBE AND AN ALLIANCE of thirty or more tribes. Wahunsenacawh, one of the great Powhatan chiefs and also later called Powhatan, united the tribes in what became known as the Powhatan Confederacy. Little is known of the early history of the tribes. It is believed that they were closely related to the Delaware, or Lenape, tribes of New Jersey, eastern Pennsylvania, and southeastern New York. Members of the confederacy lived in the Tidewater region of Virginia, the low-lying coastal

Along with many rivers and streams, the homeland of the Powhatan was dotted with coastal marshes.

plain along the west side of Chesapeake Bay. Most of the tribes ranged from the Potomac River in the north to the Nansemond River and the Great Dismal Swamp in the south.

The Spanish were the first European explorers to encounter the Powhatan. They kidnapped the chief's son and took the young man to Havana, Cuba, where he was instructed in the Spanish language and the Catholic religion. Renamed Don Luis de Valasco, he was taken to Spain and presented to King Philip II. Finally, in 1570 he returned to his homeland with several Jesuit priests. They attempted to establish a mission among the native peoples in the Virginia Tidewater. But when he found that his people were starving, Don Luis rejected Spanish culture and left the mission. The Powhatan vigorously resisted the missionaries' attempts to convert them, and early in 1571, Don Luis led a war party against the mission. The warriors destroyed the mission and killed everyone, except an altar boy named Alonso who found refuge with another tribe. Later that year, the Spanish retaliated by slaughtering thirty Powhatan warriors and recovering Alonso.

The conflict between the tribes of the Tidewater and the Europeans continued when English colonists arrived in the area in the 1580s. In 1584 and again in 1587, the English founded colonies under Sir Walter Raleigh on the islands along the coast of present-day North Carolina. The colonists explored parts of what are now southeastern Virginia and North Carolina. However, the ill-fated settlements did not survive. It is believed that the colonists were killed by native peoples still angry that the Spanish had returned and kidnapped some of them to serve as guides and interpreters. The Virginia tribes believed they should drive all Europeans from their homeland.

As the Spanish and English were struggling to establish colonies in the Chesapeake region, the great chief Powhatan (also known as the *Mamanatowick*, or Principal Chief) was striving to ally the Algonquian-speaking tribes in the Tidewater. He had inherited the right to rule six tribes, including his own tribe, the Powhatan. He defeated additional tribes and convinced others to submit to his rule. The tribes united as a confederacy for protection against their many enemies. Some historians believe that Chief Powhatan was attempting to unite the tribes as an ethnic group as well.

In 1607, colonists from London established Jamestown on the James River in eastern Virginia, the first permanent English colony in North America—and in the heart of Powhatan territory. Powhatan responded to this situation by dealing cautiously with the colonists, including their leader John Smith. Chief Powhatan asked, "Why should you take by force that from us which you can have by love? Why should you destroy us, who have provided you with food? What can you get by war?" He further explained, "I, therefore, exhort you to peaceable counsels, and, above all, I insist the guns and swords, the cause of all our jealousy and uneasiness, be removed and sent away."

Occasionally, Chief Powhatan provided the colonists with food in exchange for their support. But at other times he permitted war parties to attack them, and he encouraged warriors to steal tools and

The Powhatan first encountered the English not long after the landing at Jamestown.

weapons from the colonists. Nevertheless Chief Powhatan believed that if he helped the English fight the Spanish in Virginia then he could rely on them for protection against his Native American enemies. Only later did the chief realize that the English were competing not only with the Spanish for colonies, but also with the native peoples for land.

From 1614 to 1621 peace reigned between the Powhatan Confederacy and the English colonists. In a gesture of friendship, Chief Powhatan explained, "I am not so simple as not to know that it is better to eat good meat, be well, and sleep quietly with my women and children, to laugh and be merry with the English, and, being their friend, to have copper, hatchets, and whatever else I want, than to fly from all, to lie cold in the woods, feed upon acorns and roots . . . and to be so hunted that I cannot rest, eat, or sleep, and so, in this miserable manner, to end my miserable life; and, Captain Smith, this might soon be your fate through your rashness."

The peace outlived Chief Powhatan who died in 1618. He was succeeded by his brother Opitchapam, who turned out to be a poor leader. By 1622, Opechancanough, another of Powhatan's brothers, had become *weroance*, or chief, of the confederacy. Opechancanough, who had been a chief of the Pamunkey for many years, strongly opposed the English. He devised a strategy to drive the English completely out of his people's homeland. On March 22, 1622, the Powhatan made a daring surprise attack on the colonists. In what became known as the Massacre of 1622, they killed about one fourth of the colonists. The subsequent fighting lasted for nearly a decade, relieved with brief truces only when the natives faced starvation or the English lacked gunpowder. Finally, in the fall of 1632, the remaining Powhatan agreed to a truce. However, the conflict soon resumed and continued until 1669. By then the confederacy was shattered and the Powhatan nearly destroyed as a people. The survivors lived in small pockets scattered over their homeland.

In 1634, the Powhatan attacked Jamestown and massacred the colonists who they viewed as intruders in their homeland.

The People and the Land

The Powhatan made their home on the coastal plains and forests of what is now Virginia. Here, sandwiched between the cold of the north and the heat of the south, the climate was fairly mild. The nearby Atlantic Ocean also helped to soften the seasons, bringing cool breezes in the summers and the temperate winds in the winter. Summers could nonetheless be hot and humid, and temperatures often plunged during the winters. When the English arrived in the early 1600s, winters tended to be slightly colder than today but not enough to freeze the streams and rivers. People often enjoyed stretches of long pleasant weather in the spring and autumn. There was usually ample rainfall, yet occasionally the region suffered from droughts, as well as intense storms. In late summer fierce hurricanes sometimes swept up the coast.

The land on which the Powhatan once lived rises gradually from the ocean—from fifteen feet above sea level along the coast to an elevation of almost two hundred feet ninety miles inland. Most of the region, notably the Chesapeake Bay and James River valley, is in a low, coastal plain of peninsulas, numerous inlets, and rivers. The major rivers include the Potomac, the largest and longest in the region, the Rappahannock, and several others, whose tributaries reach inland like so many fingers. At the mouths of the many streams and rivers the tides regularly spill into the salt marshes and flow up the estuaries.

Although the Powhatan did not live on the shore, they often camped there to fish and gather shellfish. The blend of low ground, numerous rivers and streams, and the rhythm of the tides mixing salt and freshwater provided a rich habitat for a wide variety of plants and animals. The varied landscape includes beaches and drifting dunes. There are dune forests and marshes—both salt water and freshwater—along with swamps of juniper and cypress trees. The tough grasses of the beach give way to live oaks, Spanish oaks, loblolly pines, and American holly trees, as well as persimmon trees and grape vines.

The dune forest includes loblolly and yellow pines, live, laurel and Spanish oaks, black locust, and pignut hickory. Here, the Powhatan often gathered hickory nuts, along with persimmons, blackberries, and chickasaw plums. Flowing in the breeze, grasses and rushes blanketed the saltwater and freshwater marshes. Saltwater marshes provided an abundance of food, including sand fiddlers, a kind of land crab, oysters, and clams. The Powhatan found both quahogs, a hard-shelled clam, and maninose, a soft-shelled clam, as well as oysters in the saltmarsh. They also caught fish and hunted ducks that stopped there during migrations. In freshwater marshes, they dug the roots of cattails, arrow arum, broad-leaved arrowhead, and golden club, and harvested mussels.

Another kind of low, coastal forest, the pine barrens, included stands of loblolly and yellow pines. But the poor soil supported sparse vegetation and game, and the Powhatan seldom foraged and never built their villages there. Instead they established their villages farther inland in the mixed forests of sweet gum and oaks. Southern red, white, Spanish, willow, and cow oak also grew in these forests,

A mong the sedges and grasses of the low-lying marshlands, the Powhatan hunted ducks and gathered shellfish.

as did tall red maples, tulip trees, black walnut, pignut hickory, and hackberry. Red cedar, red mulberry, sassafras, dogwood, and many other small trees formed the understory. Here, the Powhatan collected blueberries, fruit, and medicinal plants, such as white trillium for snakebite and trumpet honeysuckle for coughs and sore throats.

The cypress and juniper swamps supported elms, maple, sycamore, black gum, and several kinds of oaks, notably water oaks. The abundance of mast, or acorns, provided food for many animals, and the men often hunted here, especially for white-tailed deer and black bear. Some of these North American animals were unknown to the English who adapted Powhatan names for them, such as raccoon and opossum. The land abounded in squirrels, rabbits, woodchucks, and skunks as well. Muskrats, beavers, river otters, and mink lived in or along the edges of the water. Red and gray foxes and wolves preyed upon many of these animals. Frogs, toads, lizards, and snakes, including moccasin, rattlesnake, and copperhead, slithered through the water or hid among the canes.

Many birds, including the robin and the cardinal which were new to the English, enlivened the forest with their flash of colors and pleasant songs. There were also the Carolina parakeet and the passenger pigeon, both now extinct. Owls and hawks swooped down upon mice and rabbits while herons waded the shallows, and gulls and terns flitted along the shore. Of all these birds, the Powhatan most often hunted wild turkeys. They also caught quail, mourning doves, grouse, and passenger pigeons. Of the waterbirds, they hunted Canada geese and many kinds of ducks, including mallards, teal, and canvasbacks.

The Powhatan caught and ate many kinds of freshwater fish—largemouth bass, smallmouth bass, crappie, yellow perch, channel catfish, brown bullheads, pickerel, and gar, along with bluegill and pumpkinseeds. During spring runs, they fished for eels, shad, herring, and occasionally huge sturgeon. In brackish waters, they fished for striped bass and white perch. In salt water, they caught Atlantic croaker, silver perch, spotted sea trout, kingfish, bluefish, and many others. Blessed with a mild climate, lush forests, and an abundance of wildlife, the Powhatan usually enjoyed a bountiful food supply.

2. Towns

Settling in
small towns, the
Powhatan cleared
land in the
forest and built
dome-roofed
homes covered
with mats.

THE POWHATAN SETTLED IN TOWNS ALONG RIVERS AND STREAMS, FULL AND wide enough to offer them routes of travel in their dugout canoes. If the stream was brackish—a blend of salt and freshwater—they would place the town near a large spring to have an ample supply of freshwater. Some of the rivers flowing through their territory, including the Pamunkey and the Rappahannock, are today named for Powhatan tribes.

When choosing a town site, the Powhatan looked for a location on high ground that would not be flooded in the spring. The site also had to have a good view of the river, so the town could more easily defend itself against surprise attacks. There needed to be fertile soil nearby for garden plots and fields. Powhatan towns varied in size from two to a hundred dwellings, but most had only a handful of houses. One English observer noted that the largest towns had twenty to thirty houses. Numerous settlements dotted the region. Not following any regular plan, houses stood among the fields and groves. The underbrush of the surrounding forest was cleared, because people needed to gather firewood and keep an unobstructed view of approaching enemies.

Some towns were surrounded by a fence of sharpened wooden poles about ten to twelve feet high. Known as a palisade, this fence offered protection from enemy attacks. The palisade had one narrow entrance that could be readily defended. In larger towns, only the most important buildings were enclosed within the palisade. Thomas Hariot, an Englishman who journeyed through Powhatan territory and published a book about his experience in 1590, described one

For defense
against enemy
attack, towns were
sometimes encircled
by a palisade, a wall
of vertical posts with
sharpened points.
Engraving by
Theodor de Bry.

town that was not enclosed within a palisade. In this town, known as
Secota, the houses lined a central street bordered by fields, with other
dwellings scattered about the town.

Built in the style of an Algonquian wigwam, the Powhatan house
was known as yihakan (YEE-ha-cahn). The houses varied in size, but
each usually had just one room and held six to twenty people.
Houses were made by bending poles of green wood and covering

*P*owhatan dwellings had no windows. The only light came from an entrance at the end and a fire burning in the middle of the floor.

them with sheets of bark or mats woven from marsh reeds. Women first cut saplings, removed the branches, and peeled the bark. Shoving the poles into the ground, each about a foot apart, they bent them until the other ends could be stuck into the ground. They tied the poles with twine made from roots or strips of white oak, then sheathed the frame with woven mats or sheets of bark. Three to four feet wide and eight to ten feet long, the mats or sheets of bark were strapped down with cords and small poles.

On hunting trips, women went ahead to set up temporary shelters. Bending straight, supple branches, they made a circular, dome-shaped frame and covered it with mats. In towns, they built two kinds of houses: oblong houses with sloping sides and a single doorway, and long, rectangular buildings with an entrance at either end. The larger structures, or longhouses, also had straight walls, most often covered with bark, with mat roofs, because they were intended as permanent buildings. They could be fifty to sixty feet long, with some houses up to eighty to a hundred feet in length. Houses and other town buildings had to be repaired or rebuilt as people moved to new locations.

People placed a mat over the doorway. If they were going to be away for a long time, they braced logs against the mats to keep animals out. They left a hole in the roof for the smoke rising from the cooking hearths in the middle of the room. With a fire always burning, the interior of the longhouse stayed quite warm, but the air was always thick with smoke. Women also had a hearth outside the house where they prepared meals during warm weather.

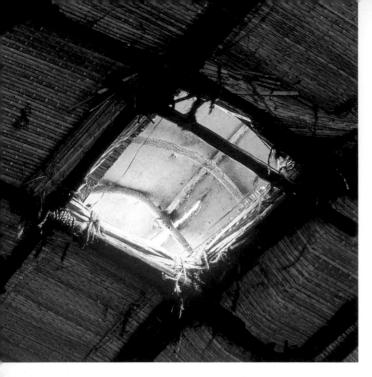

Smoke rose from cooking fires, collected under the high ceiling, and eventually drifted out a hole in the roof.

Powhatan houses generally did not have windows. During the hot summer, people removed some of the mats or rolled up the bottom edges, so cool breezes could flow through the house. However, Robert Beverley wrote in 1705 that at least some dwellings had windows. "Their windows are little holes left open for the passage of the Light, which in bad weather they stop with shutters of the same bark, opening the leeward windows for air and light."

Built along the inside walls, low platforms about a foot high served as beds at night and workplaces during the day. The platforms were covered with mats and animal skins. Clothes and other belongings, such as weapons and fishing gear, were kept in the house.

The town included a larger, more prominent dwelling for the chief and his family. The town also had a temple where people worshipped. The temple was often built separate from the houses on a hill or ridge overlooking the town. Made of the same materials as family dwellings and laid out east to west, the temple was one of the larger structures—between sixty and one hundred feet long. The temple also served as a tomb for the tribe's chiefs where their dried bodies were guarded by wooden figures representing the spirits. A priest, known as a kwiocos, kept a fire burning continuously near the

*P*eople safely stored their belongings in pots and baskets along the inside walls of their homes.

eastern entrance. Temples could also be used as storerooms by the chief. Here, food and tribute from other tribes were watched over by the god known as Okeus and the priests.

The Powhatan also constructed sweat lodges in their villages for religious rituals. They retired within the sweat lodges to purify the body and the spirit. Towns usually had an open clearing surrounded by poles as well. As large fires burned through the night, people held lively feasts as they sang and danced around the poles.

It is believed that among the Powhatan there were class distinctions between nobles and common people. When a chief died, his next oldest brother by the same mother or the children of his oldest sister assumed his position. Both men and women could inherit the position, and some women became leaders known as *weroansqua*. Families, especially the wives of a chief or wealthy man were held in high esteem. Waited upon by servants, these wives wore fine jewelry and clothes decorated with pearls. They were not required to do any work—other women undertook the countless chores of managing the household.

The Powhatan followed a daily and seasonal cycle of tasks that were clearly divided between women and men. Women cared for their children, built houses, and gathered firewood. They collected and prepared fruits, berries, and plants for food and medicine. They tanned deer and other animal hides, dyed the skins, and fashioned them into clothing, moccasins, blankets, and bags. They often decorated the finished clothing with beadwork. They also made household items, such as needles and spoons, from animal bones,

The Powhatan also cleared ceremonial space in the forest, which they encircled with wooden posts that bore carved faces.

shells, and wood. They did most of the work tending the corn, tobacco, and other crops. They harvested and ground the corn, then cooked all the meals. Accompanying men on long hunting trips, they also toted supplies, built temporary shelters, and carried the game back to the town.

After deerskins were tanned, they were fashioned into a variety of warm winter wear.

Men devoted themselves to fishing, hunting, and fighting, as well as holding councils and ceremonies. They made most of the weapons and tools needed for work and warfare, including bows and arrows, wooden clubs, and tree bark shields. Warfare was a way of life for the Powhatan and other native peoples, and the men were often preparing for an impending battle. They made dugout canoes and weirs, a kind of dam for catching fish. They cleared fields and helped to construct the large, permanent dwellings. These tasks required a great deal of effort, but also allowed the men to rest from their trips to hunt, trade, or engage in warfare. From late spring through early autumn they often fished, especially during spawning runs. During the winter, they left the town on hunting trips.

The Powhatan Confederacy

When Chief Powhatan became leader he inherited six tribes: Arrohateck, Appamatuck, Mattaponi, Pamunkey, Powhatan, and Youghtanund. All of these tribes lived within fifty miles of present-day Richmond, Virginia. Through force and trickery he managed within a few years of the arrival of the English in 1607 to build a great confederacy of thirty or more tribes in the Virginia Tidewater region. Some tribes living farther away on the Rappahannock and Potomac Rivers also became part of the confederacy, but they were not as strongly allied as those tribes located nearer the original group of allies.

Chief Powhatan assigned land to the weroances of the thirty or so major towns under his rule. The members of each tribe were allowed to hunt, fish, and gather only on this land. A local weroance, who might govern one or more towns, held great power over his people. Yet every weroance was still subject to Chief Powhatan. People looked upon Chief Powhatan as their primary leader and almost as a divine spirit. They were very fearful of him and offered gifts to their weroance so he in turn could pay tribute to Chief Powhatan. Captain

THE POWHATAN CONFEDERACY IN THE EARLY SEVENTEENTH CENTURY

MARYLAND

VIRGINIA

Rappahannock River

Potomac River

Rappahannock

Pamunkey River

Mataponi River

Youghtanund

Pamunkey

Mattaponi

York River

CHESAPEAKE BAY

ATLANTIC OCEAN

James River

Chickahominy

Arrohateck

Appomatox River

Powhatan

JAMESTOWN

Chiskiack

Kecoughtan

Appamatuck

James River

Nansemond

This map shows the locations of the tribes that made up the Powhatan Confederacy in the 1600s.

John Smith observed that Powhatan had become very wealthy from the tribute he received.

Chief Powhatan had many wives, but he did not live with all of them at the same time. He divorced some and took new ones, yet he still had to support all his wives and children. Whenever he wanted another wife, he sent his chief men to find the loveliest young women. Then he made his selection and offered the family payment. With his wives and many children, Chief Powhatan was waited upon by servants and guarded by forty to fifty warriors. He also surrounded himself with priests and loyal friends.

The weroances held great power over the people in their towns, yet over them all Powhatan was considered the supreme leader. He could punish anyone who offended him. John Smith noted that even Powhatan's frown caused people to tremble with fear. Punishments ranging from severe beatings to death were meted out for various offenses. If a person stole from another tribe member the lawbreaker was punished. However, Powhatan did not consider it wrong to steal from other tribes or the English, whose valuable goods were often taken. Serious crimes such as murder were punished with torture and death by fire or clubbing.

Chief Powhatan maintained his strong rule with the aid of his family members. His three brothers, Opitchapam, Opechancanough, and Kekataugh, governed large numbers of people in the area of the Pamunkey River. His son Parahunt was responsible for the area that is now Richmond and another son, Pochins, was leader of the Kecoughtan, another tribe of the Confederacy. Although Chief

This Theodor de Bry engraving shows two weroances, powerful chiefs who governed each of the towns.

Powhatan governed the confederacy absolutely, his priests also wielded great influence over him and the other weroances. Whenever he or the weroances intended to go to war, they first consulted with the priests.

The presence of the English began to influence Chief Powhatan and the confederacy almost immediately upon their arrival. Although the great leader sought peaceful relations with the colonists, he was also wary of them. In 1607, Chief Powhatan was living at the town of Werowocomoco along the north side of the York River. However, in January 1609, he moved west to Orapax, apparently to distance himself from the colonists at Jamestown.

3. Lifeways

During the spring, summer, and autumn, the Powhatan spent much of their time gathering food to be stored for the winter.

THE POWHATAN FOLLOWED THE CYCLE OF FIVE IMPORTANT SEASONS: THE budding or blossoming of spring; the earing of the corn; the summer or time of high sun; the corn gathering or fall of the leaf; and the winter or *cohonks*, which refers to the call of the wild geese migrating back from the north. They counted the months by the cycle of the moon and named them for the activity at the time. There was the moon of stags, the corn moon, and the first and second moon of cohonks. People followed similar cycles in their daily lives, in planting and harvesting crops, as well as hunting and fishing. Woman gave birth, men became fathers, and old people told stories drawn from deep within their pasts. Children followed the example of their parents and grandparents as they grew up, married, and had families of their own.

Cycle of Life

Birth. The birth of a child was an occasion of great joy for a family. The baby was first ritually dipped in water—no matter how cold the weather. The mother then placed her baby in a cradleboard. The baby was securely tied onto the flat board with thongs. About two feet long, the cradleboard had a leather strap so the mother could carry it on her back. Occasionally, she took her baby out of the cradleboard, but for the most part the infant remained in the cradle-board until it was old enough to crawl.

Naming a male child was especially important to the Powhatan, who believed that a name reflected a man's ability as a hunter and a warrior. Shortly after birth, they held a feast for family and friends when the father announced the baby's name. As the boy grew up, his mother gave him a nickname. If the boy proved to be especially skilled as a hunter or tracker, his father might give him yet another name. If he became a great warrior, the chief might confer an honored name as a title upon the young man.

Young children wore little or no clothing. To toughen their skin to heat and cold, mothers bathed them in the river and rubbed them with paint and animal fat. When they were seven or eight years old, both girls and boys began to wear a breechcloth, a piece of buckskin drawn between the legs and tied around the waist. At about the age of ten, they began to dress in buckskin clothes like their parents.

Childhood. Children spent most of their early years learning the skills they would need to survive as adults. Girls looked after the smaller children and learned the many household chores and crafts of their mothers. Boys practiced to become hunters and warriors. A mother might require her son to shoot at a target with his bow and arrow before she gave him breakfast. Fathers often took their sons on hunting and fishing trips. Boys contributed to the food stores of the family by shooting birds, rabbits, and other small animals that invaded the cornfields and gardens. With bows and arrows, they also shot fish in the stream flowing by their town.

Children also played games. With no written language, they learned by listening to their parents and other adults in the town, especially to the storytellers who taught them their history as a people.

Fathers taught their sons how to make bows and arrows, as well as how to use them.

Coming-of-Age. Like many Native Americans, the Powhatan held a formal ceremony to mark the passage of a boy to manhood. Known as *huskanaw*, this ceremony was held when the youths were between ten and fifteen years old. The priest selected about fifteen boys and painted their bodies for this special occasion. The young men sat under a tree and were then led one by one between two rows of men as they struck them with sticks. After the boys had run this gauntlet, they were "cast on a heap in a valley, as dead." Although referred to as a "sacrifice of children," the ceremony was meant to mold the boys into men. A group of young warriors then took the boys into the forest where for nine months they were kept in seclusion. They were allowed only an intoxicating drink which took away their senses for a period of eighteen to twenty days. Some young men did not live through this ordeal. Upon their return to the town, the youths took their place as men in the tribe. They were given new names and allowed to marry.

By the age of ten, girls dressed like their mothers and the other women in apronlike skirts. Young women were regarded as adults when they were old enough to have children. They received a new name at this time. Chief Powhatan nicknamed his favorite daughter Pocahontas, which possibly means "little wanton." Her birth name was Matoaka, but her adult name was Amonute. Like the boys, girls prepared for their lives as adults. They helped the women with daily work around the house and town, so that they would become good wives and mothers when they had their own families.

Marriage. Powhatan men could have more than one wife—in fact, as many as they could afford. A man with the greatest wealth, often the most copper or beads, had the largest number of wives. A weroance often had many wives, and parents were honored if their daughter married a chief. A man frequently took several wives to insure that he would have many children to care for him in old age. However, a weroance would have only one child with each wife. Once she had given birth, she left the household with enough copper and beads to support herself and the baby. When the child reached a certain age, it was taken from the mother and raised by the weroance.

If a man was fond of a woman, he presented her with game, fish, or fowl to impress her with his ability as a hunter. If the parents allowed him to court her, he had to promise to provide for her. Often,

Once the marriage price was agreed upon, the bride's family was often presented with a rich array of furs.

he gave her a token of betrothal in the presence of her parents and arranged for a marriage price with her father or other relatives. When they reached agreement on the number of furs, deerskins, and other valuable goods to be exchanged, both families celebrated. The parents then brought their daughter to the man's home—sometimes hundreds of miles away—for the wedding. The bride's father or a close friend placed her hands in those of her intended. The groom's father then took a long string of beads, measured out an arm's length, and broke it over the couple's heads. He gave the beads to the bride's father after which everyone enjoyed a great wedding feast.

The Powhatan usually married at a young age. When a young woman was thirteen, she might take a husband. After being accepted as an adult, a young man might marry when he was fifteen. Marriage was considered sacred, but divorce was permitted. When a couple separated, their marriage ties were dissolved and each was allowed to marry again. If they disagreed about the custody of the children, the children were divided equally between the parents, with the man having first choice.

Death. The Powhatan believed that the souls of the dead went to the land of the spirits. They took special care in preserving the bodies of their leaders in the temple. Bodies of other people were buried in individual graves. Later, in a special ceremony, the bones of many people were dug up and reburied together in an earthen mound. Bundles of bones, some from cremated bodies, were also reburied in pits with grave goods. Sites of these mass graves have been found on the Potomac, Rappahannock, and York Rivers.

Upon death, the body was carefully prepared for burial. With sharpened sticks, people dug the grave. Wrapped in skins and mats, the body was placed in the hole upon a bed of sticks with jewels and other grave goods and then covered with earth. Women, blackened their faces with charcoal, sat in their homes, wailing and howling, as they mourned the loss of their loved one.

Another kind of burial involved wrapping the body in mats and placing it on a scaffold about ten to twelve feet above the ground. Family members grieved and threw beads to the poor who were gathered there. The mourners then went to the home of the deceased's family where they sang, danced, and feasted for the rest of the day. After the body had completely decomposed, they took the bones from the scaffold, wrapped them in another mat, and placed them in a house. Over time, the house fell to ruins and the bones were left buried in the debris.

Weroances and other notable people were treated with their own distinctive funerary rituals. The body was first disembowelled and dried on a wooden frame. Copper and pearl jewelry was hung on the neck and arms. The body cavity was filled with copper beads and covered with skins, hatchets, and other ritual objects. Wrapped in mats, the body was then placed on a platform under an arch made of mats in a special temple. Here, among statues of Powhatan gods, the bodies of the chiefs were laid out in orderly rows with their wealth placed in baskets at their feet. Within the temple, priests watched over the bodies.

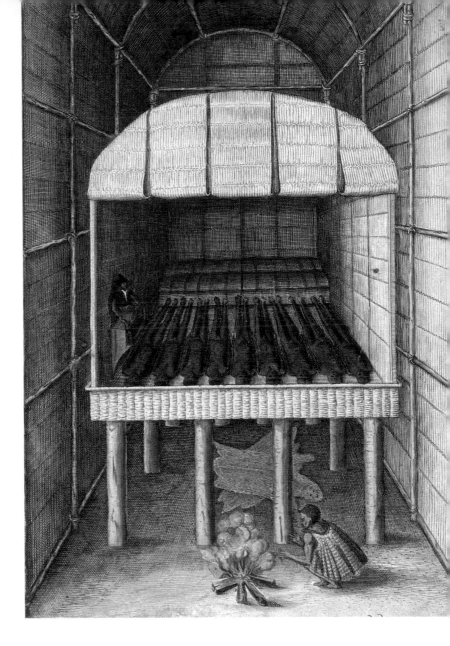

As depicted in this de Bry engraving, the Powhatan placed the bodies of dead chiefs on platforms in special temples.

According to the origin story of the Patawomeck, or Potomac, upon death, people ate all manner of fruit—mulberries, strawberries, and plums—as they journeyed toward the rising sun, the home of Great Hare. On the way, they encountered a goddess. The doors of her home were always open. She gave them luscious fruits, tasty green corn, and walnuts from which they drank a delicious milk. Refreshed, the people continued to the east, where they met their ancestors. Singing and dancing, the ancestors ate fruit, and the recently deceased joined them in their happy life with Great Hare. When they became old and died in the spirit world, they returned to the earth again, repeating the cycle.

Gathering and Gardening

Having lived on the coastal plain of Virginia for many generations, the Powhatan learned a great deal about gathering fruit and growing crops in that region. They knew which wild plants could be eaten or used as medicine and which were poisonous. Women gathered roots, bark, fruit, and berries from the forests and marshes. Herbs were used as flavoring in meals. Among the medicinal foods was sassafras tea, made from the tree's boiled roots. Southern snakeroot, goldenseal, and wild strawberry were also used as medicines.

When food was plentiful, people enjoyed a hearty and healthy diet. However, they were always at the mercy of the weather. Occasional droughts or unseasonably cold weather during the growing season often drastically reduced the food supply. The most difficult time was usually late winter and early spring when stored foods ran low and plants had not yet sprouted or berries ripened. Then they often ate the inner bark and twigs of trees, such as pine, maple, and willow. They also cooked the sap of maple and hickory trees to make a sweet syrup and crumbly brown sugar.

From late spring until first frost, the land abounded with fruits and berries, including grapes, strawberries, gooseberries, raspberries, huckleberries, mulberries, persimmons, cherries, and plums. The Powhatan especially liked mulberries. Nuts and other seeds were also important foods. Women gathered acorns, hickory nuts, chestnuts, walnuts, pecans, and other nuts. Acorns had to be dried and boiled to remove their bitter taste. The Powhatan also used seeds in making bread and broth. They may also have enjoyed wild leeks, which are now sometimes known as ramps. They probably also collected onions and various wild greens, including lettuce.

Women dug roots and tubers, such as Indian cucumber and groundnuts, which were eaten raw or boiled. They gathered Chinaroot, a rhubarblike plant, which they chopped into small pieces, pounded, and strained with water to make a thick jelly. Sometimes they dried this jelly into a powder, which could be stored for a long time. Men often took the powder with them on journeys. When they were hungry, they added water and cooked the mixture into a nutritious food.

People also relied on the wilderness to provide materials for tools, clothing, and household items. They obtained red dye for painting their faces, bodies, and clothing from bloodroot. From goldenseal they made a yellow dye, and wild indigo provided an excellent shade of deep blue. They made strong cords from milkweed and dogbane, a plant also known as Indian hemp. Women gathered canes along rivers and streams for making baskets and mats, beds, and other household items. Tree bark and reeds, along with corn husks were woven into baskets. Seeds were used as beads for necklaces. Women also dug a kind of reddish clay, which they used not only in pottery making, but as a dressing for wounds.

The Powhatan also cultivated fields. To make new fields, the men followed a slash-and-burn method to clear the trees and underbrush. They killed the trees by chopping away the bark near the roots or burning the base of the tree. They burned the leaves and branches to get rid of the debris. The ashes helped to fertilize the soil. The fol-

Clay was unearthed and turned into a variety of pots used for storing corn and other foods.

lowing season, they dug up the soil around the dead trees and planted crops. The Powhatan tilled the field until the soil became exhausted, then they moved to other land. In previously cultivated fields, as the days warmed in the spring, both men and women labored to loosen the soil with a wooden tool similar to a hoe. They removed and burned any weeds and old cornstalks.

Planting usually began in April and was not completed until mid-June, but most of the work was undertaken in May. Squatting on the ground, women used a planting stick, a hand tool about a foot long and four or five inches wide, to make holes in the soil about a yard apart. They dropped kernels of corn and bean seeds in each hole, then covered them. They planted squash, pumpkins, sunflowers, and other vegetables between the holes. As the clumps of plants grew in the heat of summer, they hilled the corn and beans to form low mounds. Stationed in a platform in the field, a child often guarded the fields to keep rabbits, deer, raccoons, and birds from nibbling the tender green shoots and munching on the juicy ears of corn. They began to pick the mature ears of corn in August and continued to harvest the crops as they ripened until late October.

The Powhatan grew several kinds of corn. One was a variety like popcorn that grew three or four feet high and ripened early. Flint or hominy corn had large, smooth kernels in several colors—red, yellow, white, and blue. Dent or flour corn was also grown. Women dried the kernels, then ground them into a meal or coarse flour. The yellow meal, which kept fairly well, was baked in breads and boiled in soups.

Women also grew peas in the gardens near their houses. Dried beans and peas could be stored for long periods of time. These foods were then boiled, often with corn and meat. Sometimes, women pounded the dried beans and peas in a wooden mortar, and used the meal in breads. Sunflower seeds added flavor to breads and broths. The Powhatan also dried strips of pumpkin and squash, which were later baked in hot ashes. Gourds were also grown and the dried shells made into water jugs, dishes, and ladles.

The Powhatan grew tobacco in small plots. They carefully tended the plants and harvested the leaves, which were then dried and shredded. Men carried tobacco in pouches and smoked it in clay and stone pipes. They offered tobacco to visitors to their towns as a sign of welcome and goodwill. However, they primarily used tobacco in

Women raised gourds and fashioned the dried shells into ladles and other household utensils.

The Powhatan also tended tobacco plants. After the leaves were harvested, they were dried and shredded for use in ceremonies.

religious ceremonies. They believed that the spirits loved tobacco, which also grew in the land of the dead. They sprinkled tobacco to calm turbulent waters or cast some in the air following an escape from danger. They burned the sacred leaves as offerings and sprinkled tobacco over a new fish weir for good luck. Native tobacco had a strong taste, and for casual smoking the Powhatan came to favor the milder West Indian varieties imported by the English.

Hunting and Fishing

The Powhatan hunted the forests and fished the streams of their homeland. They stalked game in meadows and marshes and fished along the beaches and bays. With its many swamps, inlets, and sounds, the coastal region abounded in wildlife. The Chesapeake Bay to the north and the Great Dismal Swamp to the south were especially rich sources of fish, shellfish, and birds. As one traveled inland,

Men kept their arrows in a quiver made from animal skin, bark, or the stems of reeds gathered from nearby marshes.

vast stretches of forest blanketing the rolling hills and valleys were home to deer, bear, and other wildlife.

Highly skilled hunters, men journeyed on foot over woodland trails or paddled their dugout canoes up rivers and through the dank green forest. They knew the land well and readily traveled hundreds of miles over well-worn trails. The men were superb trackers and had great stamina and patience. Although women often accompanied them to set up camp and haul meat back to the town, the men and older boys did the actual hunting.

To bring down game, small and large, hunters mostly relied on bows and arrows. Deer were a major a source of food and materials for making tools and clothing. Hunting alone, a man occasionally wore a deerskin over his head so he could artfully stalk and approach his prey. Other times, the Powhatan hunted in groups of as many as three hundred men. Traveling inland for two or three days, they built many small fires in a circle and stationed hunters in between the fires. Other members of the party pursued and killed the deer, elk, bear, and other game trapped within the circle of fire. Another approach involved driving the deer to a narrow point of land and into the river, where men in dugouts easily killed them.

Black bears, which provided huge amounts of greasy meat, were an especially welcome trophy in the long, hard winters when game was often in short supply. The lumbering creatures were also a vital source of fat which women stored in skins and used in cooking. People also smeared bear grease in their hair and over their skin. The skins made warm coats and bedding. Men would often chase bears

Poling dugouts, men fished with nets, spears, and weirs, a kind of trap made of reeds or sticks placed in the water. Engraving by Theodor de Bry.

until they climbed a tree and then could be easily taken. Cougars and wolves were also a favorite quarry, while otters and beavers were most often trapped with snares.

Boys and men both hunted rabbits. The meat was cooked, and the skins were sewn into short, sleeveless coats called mantles. Squirrels, raccoons, and other small animals were also caught. Young boys who wanted to practice their hunting skills shot squirrels from tree branches. Game birds provided meat, eggs, and feathers. The Powhatan sometimes also ate locusts and beetles.

The men fished in the rivers, bays, and ocean. Shad were an especially important fish caught on their spawning runs up the rivers. During these annual runs, the Powhatan also caught huge sturgeon by slipping a noose around their tail. They fished with lines and hooks made from small bones or the hollow tails of crabs. They scooped fish in dip nets woven from cords. Both girls and boys speared fish in shallow water with reeds fitted with sharp points of seashell. Men and boys also shot fish with bows and arrows. Often they attached a line to the arrow if they were aiming at fish in deep water. Occasionally, they fished at night, a boy or man holding a torch while the others shot at the fish attracted to the light.

They also caught fish in two kinds of fish traps, or weirs. To make a hedge-style weir, men stuck reeds or sticks in the water to form a V shape. As the fish swam through the narrow point, people easily caught them with dip nets. The Powhatan also placed stones across rivers where the current was brisk, placing baskets in the gaps. The swift current swept the fish between the rocks and into the baskets. Other times, they left the gaps open. As the fish swam through, men easily speared them.

Making Meals

Roots from such plants as tuckahoe were pounded into flours for baking breads. Wild rice, flavored with deer fat, was also made into a tasty bread. However, the Powhatan relied primarily on corn as a

Women cooked over open fires. Here, a light meal of corn cakes and maple syrup has been prepared.

staple food. They especially liked green corn with its milky kernels, similar to the sweet corn of today. They boiled this corn in large clay pots or roasted the ears over the fire. However, the hard kernels of most corn were pounded and parched for better storage through the lean months of winter. Parched corn was made by roasting meal in hot ashes. Later it was boiled with beans. Men also carried parched cornmeal with them on long journeys. Women mixed the cornmeal with water and shaped it into loaves which they steeped in hot water and dried. They later boiled these loaves to make broths. The women

Corn and Beans

Like other Native Americans, the Powhatan ate stews and soups made with corn, beans, and other vegetables. Many of their recipes for corn and bean dishes were adopted by the settlers. Here is a modern version of a basic recipe similar to the meals eaten by the Powhatan:

Ingredients

1 chopped onion

1 sweet pepper (red, yellow, or green)

1 cup water

2 cups shelled fresh or frozen lima beans or two 16-ounce cans of lima beans

2 cups of fresh or frozen yellow corn or two 16-ounce cans of corn

2 tablespoons butter

salt and pepper to taste

Simmer all ingredients, except butter, in a large covered saucepan for twenty minutes or until lima beans are tender. Drain excess liquid, add butter, and serve hot.

Serves about eight people.

*H*ere, *in a de Bry engraving, a man is drying fish, which was placed on a rack above the fire.*

also made rockahominy, which is now known as hominy. They soaked the kernels in a solution of water and ashes before hulling and boiling them over a low fire for several hours. Fish and meat were cooked with the hominy. Sometimes, hominy was simmered in water to make a nutritious dish, now known as grits.

Meats were either boiled or roasted, while fish was usually broiled over the fire on spits or hurdles made of a framework of branches. Sometimes, meat, fish, and oysters were preserved by curing them over the smoke of a low fire. Clams and mussels were often eaten in stews thickened with cornmeal. Fruits and berries were dried on mats and stored for the long winter. Bear fat was used to flavor soups and stews.

In preparing meals, women placed a large clay pot with a round bottom on the ground. Filling the pot with water, they built a fire around the base and cooked meat, vegetables, and fruit into stews. A pot was always simmering over the fire, and people ate whenever they were hungry. The settlers at Jamestown were amazed by the large amounts of food the Powhatan were able to consume at a single meal. Sitting on woven mats, they ate from wooden bowls and platters with horn or wooden spoons. Captain John Smith noted that after Chief Powhatan had eaten, his wives brought him water in a wooden bowl to wash his hands and then dried his hands with feathers.

Clothing and Jewelry

In the fairly warm climate of Virginia, the Powhatan dressed simply. Young boys and girls usually went naked during the summer. When they were about eight years old, girls began to wear a simple breechcloth. Boys began to dress similarly when they were ten to twelve years old. Men usually wore a breechcloth made from the skin of a deer or other animal. They drew the strip of leather between their legs and tied the breechcloth around their waists with a cord or belt, allowing a flap to drape in the front and back. Men attached a leather bag decorated with shells to their belts, usually on the right side. They kept tobacco, pipes, knives, and other belongings in the bag. Women wore apronlike skirts of fringed buckskin or occasionally woven grass, that reached almost to the knees and opened at the back.

Bare from the waist up, men, women, and children smeared their bodies with bear fat mixed with dyes as a form of adornment. Blue, yellow, and white, but especially red and black were common. The grease also helped to keep them cool in summer and warm in winter and offered some protection against fleas, mosquitoes, and gnats. Priests painted their bodies half black and half red. When they went to war or prepared for games, men painted themselves to appear as fierce as possible. Women also adorned themselves with elaborate tattoos. They covered their arms, breasts, thighs, and faces with images of flowers, fruits, snakes, and other creatures.

Chiefs and other important men wore leather shirts. The wealthy also donned capes. Priests favored capes that hung down to the middle of the thigh. Draped over one shoulder, the capes left the other shoulder uncovered and the arm free. Most often, the capes were made of leather, but occasionally they were made from furs or feathers. During the winter, most people wore fur robes, leather moc-casins, and leggings. When they traveled, the Powhatan often put on moccasins to protect their feet, but otherwise they went barefoot in mild weather.

People wore their hair in a variety of styles, depending on their social class and age. They rubbed grease into their black hair to give

The Powhatan often adorned their buckskin clothing with shells, glass beads, and other ornaments.

it a nice sheen. Women served as the stylists for the men as well as for themselves. Girls and unmarried women shaved the front and sides of their heads. The remaining long hair was tied in a plait and hung down the back. Married women allowed their hair to grow long. Women often adorned their hair with flowers or feathers. Men had the right sides of their heads plucked by women who used shells as tweezers. Apparently they did not want their hair to get in the way when they were shooting arrows. They allowed the left side to grow long and cut the hair on top of their heads, from the forehead to the back of the neck, in a short, brushlike style called a roach. Sometimes, they pulled the long hair tight and tied it in a knot. In the knot, they might wear the dried hand of an enemy, a bird wing, pieces of copper, or beads. Priests shaved the sides of their head,

This de Bry engraving depicts a prominent elder in traditional winter dress with a cape drawn over his shoulder.

leaving a roach of hair down the middle. Using mussel shells as tweezers, women pulled out the men's facial hair, so they did not have beards or moustaches.

Both men and women pierced their ears and wore earrings made from shells and other materials. It was reported that men sometimes even wore a small, live snake in their ears. People also donned necklaces and bracelets made of shells, bones, stones, and seeds. Chiefs and other wealthy men often wore jewelry made of pearls and copper beads. Hammered into breastplates, pendants, headbands, and ornaments for the hair and ears, copper was highly prized. Copper chains and beads were lavished on images of the god Okeus and the bodies of deceased weroances.

Shell money, called *roanoke*, was made from mussels and other thin shells; these were shaped into discs, with a hole in the center, and carried on a string. The Powhatan also made valuable beads called *runtees*. In the early seventeenth century wampum also became a form of currency. Either purple or white, these cylindrical beads were made from various seashells including the quahog clam.

Handicrafts

Among their many tasks, women also worked at many useful crafts. They fashioned mortars from logs by burning and scraping the end to make a hole about ten to fourteen inches deep. They made the pestle by scraping down a hickory log, leaving a heavy clubbed end for weight. They used the mortar and pestle most often to pound corn into meal, but sometimes, they ground corn with a pair of stones, one rubbed against the other. They also made platters by scraping and charring hardwoods. They fashioned spoons from horn or large bivalve shells. Women also twisted fiber into cord and twine and wove baskets and mats from cornhusks, tree bark, wicker, hemp, and silk grass. They made baskets for gathering corn in the field and larger baskets in which the corn was dumped, as well as storage baskets in homes. They also wove fine sieves for sifting cornmeal.

A skilled craftsperson could turn a couple of hickory logs into a mortar and pestle in no time at all.

The Powhatan made cooking pots from clay tempered, or strengthened, with sand. Instead of turning their pots on wheels, they wound and pressed coils of clay together, gradually shaping the vessel with their fingers and then smoothing the surface of the pot with cords of twisted hemp. The finished pots were hardened over a fire. They made pots in many shapes and sizes. Some were as small as teacups; others large enough to hold several gallons of water.

Men made tools and weapons. According to John Smith, they made knife blades from split reeds. These knives were used to trim feathers to the proper shape for arrows, butcher deer and game, and cut buckskin for clothing and moccasins. The men also chipped sharp knives from stone and traded for metal knives. They turned deer antlers and bones, along with the bones of birds, especially turkeys, into pins, awls, fishhooks, chisels, and points for arrows and spears. They made scrapers from bones, stones, and shells, and drills from reeds and stones.

Axes were made by tightly fitting and gluing a wooden handle into a hole chipped in the stone. They similarly attached a deer horn to a handle to make a fearsome war club to wield in battle. The men later traded with the English for metal hatchets and axes. Weapons also included curved swords, about three feet long, made from hardwood decorated with paintings and carved designs. Other swords were set with stone edges and pieces of iron. Additional protection came from circular, bark shields.

Bows and arrows were the most important weapons for hunting and warfare. Men fashioned bows that were about five to six feet long from various woods, especially witch hazel and locust. They shaped the wooden pole with shell scrapers, and fitted the bow with a tightly twisted string of deer sinew or a strip of deerhide. They made at least two kinds of arrows. For hunting birds and squirrels, they favored straight wooden shafts tipped with a sliver of bone about two or three inches long. Made with a reed and a wooden shaft, the other kind of arrow was tipped with a turkey spur, a sharpened piece of seashell, a honed tine of a deer antler, or chipped stone points. There was not much flint where the Powhatan lived, so they used quartz or traded with other tribes for flint, which they chipped into triangular arrowheads with a flaker. Warriors always carried a flaker. Made from a

*M*en chipped razor-sharp arrowheads in various shapes and sizes.

deer antler about four to five inches long, this tool was used for chipping a sharp edge on arrowheads. They attached arrowheads and turkey feathers to the shaft with a jellylike glue made by boiling deer antlers. They kept their arrows in a quiver made from animal skin, reeds, or bark.

Men skillfully crafted boats known as dugouts. First, they felled a tree by setting a fire around the base. With stone axes, they cut the log to the desired length and removed the branches. Placing the log on forked posts, they scraped off the bark, then built small fires on top along the length of the log, to gradually burn the inside. As a hollow was formed, they cut and scraped away the charred wood with stone axes and shells. They shaped the outside so the dugout glided easily through the water.

Here a woman makes a dugout using turkey feathers to fan the coals that are slowly burning away the log. With so many bodies of water in Powhatan territory and an extensive trade network, a sturdy canoe was essential.

Warfare

War was a way of life for the Powhatan and the other tribes of the region. Chief Powhatan established his principal city inland for better defense against the Susquehannock of Maryland and Iroquoian peoples, including the Massawomecks who lived north of them. The Monacans and their allies, the Mannahoacs, were also bitter enemies of the Powhatan. Chief Powhatan eventually destroyed the towns of the Chesapeake Indians who lived near present-day Virginia Beach. Captain John Smith observed that the Powhatan did not go to war for land or goods but for revenge. They also captured women and children to replace those lost in conflicts and to increase the size of their own tribe.

However, Chief Powhatan went to war primarily to achieve greater power for himself and his empire. His brother Opechancanough later fought two wars to drive the English from Powhatan lands. When he wished to make war, Chief Powhatan held a council of weroances, advisors, friends, and priests. Powerful leaders, such as Opechancanough, were very influential in the deliberations, but everyone listened closely to the priests. It was believed that the priests, with their spiritual powers, could predict whether a campaign would be victorious. Chief Powhatan chose to attack and nearly destroy the Chesapeake Indians because the priests had told him that a great nation might arise in the east and assail his people through Chesapeake Bay.

Before they went into combat, the Powhatan painted their bodies to appear very fierce. The warriors fasted and danced to war drums

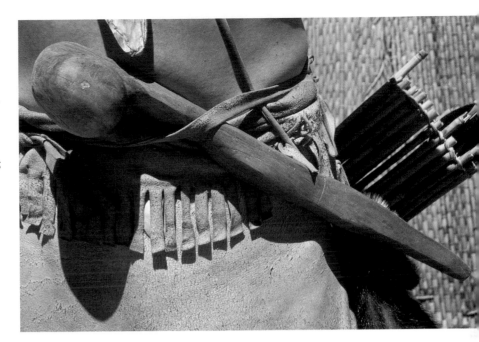

Among the weapons of the Powhatan was the war club, which warriors used against their enemies in close combat.

and prayed to the spirits for good fortune in battle. Then they went to war. Silently making their way through the forests, the warriors hoped to make a surprise attack. To avoid discovery while on the march, they separated each morning and agreed to meet at a certain place that evening. Coming together for the battle, they crept through the underbrush as they approached the enemy town. Then, swinging war clubs and shooting arrows, they swept down upon the unsuspecting people. Sometimes, Chief Powhatan employed trickery. In 1608, he sent several warriors, posing as hunters, to spend the night with the Piankatank. When the Piankatank were asleep, the visitors signaled to a large force of warriors hidden in the forest. In the ensuing massacre, only a few Piankatank warriors escaped death. The scalps of the slaughtered warriors were brought home and strung between two trees.

Fighting was brutal, with no mercy shown on either side. Captive men expected to be tortured and put to death. They showed their courage and strength by not crying out as strips of flesh were torn from their bodies. Women and children were seized and taken back to the town where they were adopted by Powhatan families or sold as slaves to other tribes. When the warriors returned from a battle, everyone in the town offered thanks in a great celebration of feasting and dancing. Those warriors who had killed the largest number of enemies were greatly honored.

Travel and Trade

When hunting or trading, the Powhatan often journeyed hundreds of miles from their town. Travelers were also welcomed as they passed through Powhatan towns. They greeted strangers from friendly tribes with courtesy, food, and drink. It was expected that the traveler graciously accept whatever was offered him, then lend an ear to an evening of conversation and storytelling.

The tribes in the Tidewater spoke similar languages, so they had little difficulty in communicating among themselves. However, in dealing with other peoples, they relied on signals, such as laying down their arms to show peaceful intentions. Spreading a mat and offering a pipe to visitors were signs of welcome. By contrast, fitting an arrow in a bow or shaking a war club indicated anger and distrust. When a man swore a solemn oath he pointed to the sun and laid his right hand upon his heart. Through simple gestures a man also told his hosts that he was hungry or sleepy.

Year after year, the Powhatan journeyed along the same narrow paths. Originally made by animals, the paths were seldom more than twenty inches wide. They chose paths on high ground or along low ridges with less underbrush and fewer deep streams to cross. They also favored trails that passed through gaps between high peaks. English settlers followed these same footpaths through the forests. In time these paths became wagon trails and, in some cases, the highways of today.

Prior to 1607, the Powhatan engaged in widespread trade with other tribes. The most desired trade items included copper, shell beads, bone objects, and occasional soapstone pipes, along with furs, tobacco, corn, and mats. The trade in marine shells for making beads extended inland far from the Atlantic and Gulf coasts. Some copper was found in Virginia, but most came from sources as far away as the Lake Superior region. Soon after the founding of Jamestown, Captain John Smith realized the need to trade with the Powhatan, especially for corn. He visited several towns along the main rivers of the Tidewater. By trading and sometimes seizing corn from the Powhatan, the colonists avoided starvation. After 1614, however, the colonists were growing enough corn to feed themselves—except on a few occasions when they were so intent on getting rich by growing tobacco for trade that they did not plant enough corn. During this time, the Powhatan often did not have enough of this important staple. Having once helped the struggling colonists, they now had to

The shells of oysters and quahogs, which the Powhatan harvested along the coast, were a valuable commodity in the confederacy's brisk trade with other nations.

trade beaver and otter pelts, and even their ancestral lands, for corn grown by the colonists.

Animal furs became so valuable that the colonists were willing to trade guns and ammunition to the Powhatan for them. At first, only beaver and otter pelts were in demand, but after 1620 the Virginia Company, which had founded Jamestown, began to offer high prices for marten, wildcat, fox, and muskrat skins. In an effort to keep the Powhatan from acquiring weapons, the colonial leaders began in 1617 to regulate trade with the Native Americans. As punishment, anyone who traded guns to the Virginia natives received the death penalty. By 1624, licenses to trade with the Indians had to be obtained from the governor. These regulations were revised during the second and third quarters of the century. Penalties for disregarding the laws included forfeiture of property, life imprisonment, and even death.

Trade with the Powhatan varied, depending on whether they were on peaceful terms with the colonists. An ambitious colonist named William Claiborne organized trading parties, offering the natives glass beads, copper rings, copper belts, iron and copper bracelets, and cloth. The colonists also exchanged such goods as pipes, copper kettles, needles, pins, scissors, fishhooks, and metal knives and hatchets. They usually sought furs in return but sometimes traded for dugouts, pottery, baskets, mats, wooden platters, corn, and game. Another colonist, Henry Fleet, was captured in 1623 on a trading mission and held captive for four years. During his captivity he acquired a great knowledge of the Powhatan. After friends ransomed him, he became a very successful trader.

In 1645 and 1646, four forts were constructed in Powhatan territory: Fort Royal at the Pamunkey River, Fort Charles at the falls of the James River, Fort James at the ridge of the Chickahominy River, and Fort Henry at the falls of the Appomattox River. Although built for defensive purposes, these forts soon became bustling centers of trade. Trade regulations continued to be tightened over the remainder of the century. In 1656, a law was passed that required native peoples to have "tickets" to hunt, fish, and gather within the bounds of what had once been ancestral land but was now colonial territory. Later, in 1661, copper or silver badges engraved with the name of their town were given to tribal chiefs. Any Powhatan who entered English territory without a badge was imprisoned until the weroance ransomed him.

4.Beliefs

The Powhatan honor the sun,
which they believed was
created by the great god
known as Ahone.

THE POWHATAN BELIEVED IN MANY GODS. OKEUS, THEIR PRINCIPAL GOD, had introduced evil to the world. To please this god, priests admonished the people to offer sacrifices. The Powhatan also told of creator-gods, and the early accounts written by English travelers and colonists suggest that the beliefs may have varied from town to town. Among the Patawomeck Great Hare was said to have made the world. Elsewhere a major god known as Ahone was recognized. Ahone created the gods, who helped him make and care for the earth. He made the sun, the moon, and the stars. On the earth, he made the water and the land. He then created a woman who gave birth to the first people of the world. As the colonist William Strachey stated, this god "makes the sun to shine, creating the moone and starrs his companyons, great powers, and which dwell with him, and by whose virtues and influences the under earth is tempered, and brings forth the fruicts according to her seasons." The Powhatan generally held the sun in great reverence. They also worshipped such forces in nature as lightning and thunder, and fire and water. If the people wanted more or less rain they made offerings of copper or beads.

The gods often assumed human form, and the Powhatan carved wooden statues of them, which then became divine spirits. Temples, or *quiocosin* houses, were built to house one to three statues. People worshipped and made offerings to these representations of the gods. Wooden posts erected on ceremonial occasions and carved with women's faces may have represented a deity or class of deities. Stone statues were also sometimes placed in forests and fields. The people revered all the gods and taught their children to respect them.

The Powhatan believed that spirits dwelled in the surrounding forest. Every weroance's territory had its own temple to honor them.

Families offered a prayer of thanksgiving before each meal. People also prayed on special occasions, such as when they prepared for war.

The Powhatan were deeply religious people, and the territory of every weroance had a temple. About 18 to 20 feet wide and 30 to 100 feet long, the building was shaped like a loaf, with a door facing east. In the west end, a special chamber was partitioned from the rest of the temple. Here, the bodies of dead weroances were placed on a platform several feet above the ground. Within the sacred chamber, they also placed statues of Okee or Okeus. Wooden posts carved to resemble the faces of dead leaders also stood in this chamber.

Chief Powhatan's primary temple was a place known as Uttamussak, most likely on the eastern side of the Pamunkey River. Seven priests usually lived in this temple and watched over the tombs and sacred objects. The temple was considered so holy that only weroances and priests were allowed to enter. When going up and down the river, people tossed a piece of copper, white beads, or other offering in the water as they passed by. One, two, or occasionally three priests watched over an ordinary temple. They always kept a fire burning near the eastern end.

There was clear ranks among the priests. Older, experienced priests enjoyed greater respect. Conjurers belonged to a lower class of priests. A weroance considered himself fortunate if he had a chief priest in his town, beloved of the gods, who understood the mysteries of the supernatural. Priests had great influence over both the people and the weroances. Chiefs often consulted with them before making any important decision.

*F*aces adorned the ceremonial circle of wooden posts. The carvings may have represented Powhatan gods in human form.

Feasts and Festivals

The Powhatan enjoyed many rituals and ceremonies, but they did not have special religious holidays. Prominent visitors to a town were formally welcomed with a feast. A pipe was filled with tobacco and bluish smoke soon curled upward. People danced and sang to the rhythm of drums, gourd rattles, and reed flutes.

Most feasts included offerings to the gods and centered on the seasons and other significant events such as the return of wild fowl,

People often gathered for religious ceremonies, which included offerings to the gods to celebrate a bountiful harvest or a victory in battle.

the ripening of berries, the harvest of crops, as well as victory in battle. People rejoiced when they had plentiful crops of corn and beans, and they celebrated when the hunters returned with meat. During big hunts and fish runs, many people from different tribes and towns often came together. People not only caught up on news, but enjoyed plenty of good food in these gatherings. During the greatest celebration held during the corn harvest people sang, danced, and played sports for several days.

War could be an occasion for joy or sorrow—as well as apprehension. Before they left, men sought the blessing of their priests. They fasted and danced to the beating of war drums. If the war party returned victorious, with few losses, the warriors were greeted with a great feast. The warriors offered gifts of tobacco or deer fat to the gods, and captives were tortured and eventually killed. However, when a defeated war party returned, women mourned the loss of their loved ones by wailing and painting their faces black.

Games and Gambling

The Powhatan enjoyed playing many games, including the widespread Native American stickball game, which was adopted by French-Canadian settlers and became the modern-day lacrosse. Southern tribes, including the Powhatan, played the game with two wooden sticks. Each stick had a loop at the end with a pocket of woven leather strips for catching the ball. Groups from towns or tribes competed against each other on a large field with two goals. Each side tried to carry the ball to its goal.

*C*hiefs needed to be more than wise leaders. Warriors worthy of leadership often distinguished themselves on the playing fields first.

Men also played a game, similar to soccer, in which they could use only their feet to move the ball down the field. This game required considerable speed, endurance, and agility. Young boys and women enjoyed another kind of sport in which they made goals like the men, but did not fight or tackle other players. Men also played a game in which they dropped and kicked a small ball made of animal skin. The man who kicked the ball the farthest won the game.

Chunkey, another game popular throughout the Southeast, was occasionally played by the Powhatan. Chunkey was played with a stone roller and slender poles about eight to ten feet long. Men painstakingly shaped and polished a stone into a small disc about three to five inches in diameter and about one and one-quarter inches thick. Two players usually competed against each other in this game. As the stone was rolled along a carefully smoothed ground, each player threw his pole. The player who hit or struck nearer to the stone roller won the contest. A player could also knock his opponent's pole away from the stone.

People also loved to play a counting game with sticks. Each player snatched up a handful of sticks or straws. The object of the game was to count an opponent's sticks as fast as possible. Whoever finished counting an opponent's sticks first won the game. Men enjoyed a card game, similar to the modern game of poker, in which they used cards made of split reeds. In this lively competition, they often gambled away their possessions—weapons, clothes, and other valuables. As William Strachey observed, "They will play at this for their bowes and arrowes, their copper beads, hatchets, and leather coats."

5. Changing World

For hundreds of years, the Powhatan thrived in towns along the rivers and streams of what is now Virginia.

"Bearded men should come & take away their Country & that there should none of the original Indians be left, within an hundred & fifty years."

—prediction of a Powhatan priest

Not long after the Powhatan signed a treaty with the English colonists in 1632, the Powhatan tribe, from which the alliance had taken its name, disappeared. It is believed that the tribe possibly moved upriver into the hill country, away from the colonists at Jamestown. From 1644 to 1646, war broke out, and Opechancanough was killed, which effectively destroyed the Powhatan Confederacy. Reduced to small, isolated groups, the tribes were overwhelmed and easily defeated by the settlers pouring into Virginia. After the subjugation of the Powhatan, only small pockets of native peoples remained in the Tidewater region. In the early 1600s, the Powhatan confederacy had between 3,900 and 10,400 people, according to estimates by John Smith and William Strachey. By 1669, the population had plunged to 2,900 due to warfare, starvation, and disease.

The rapid decline of the Powhatan way of life may possibly be explained through the life of a single person—Pocahontas. Although the life of the Powhatan princess has become the subject of a well-known myth, she actually lived through the drastic changes that swept away the native peoples of Virginia in less than half a century.

The Powhatan way of life changed dramatically after English colonists arrived on the shores of their ancestral homeland.

Pocahontas

Pocahontas was the daughter of Chief Powhatan. Born around 1595 to one of Powhatan's many wives, she was named Matoaka, although she became well known as Pocahontas, meaning Little Wanton, because of her playful nature.

Pocahontas likely first saw people of European descent in May 1607 when the English arrived in Virginia and established the colony of Jamestown. She achieved fame for saving the life of Captain John Smith, the leader of the struggling colony, although the story has been romanticized. Smith was leading an expedition in December 1607 that was attacked by Powhatan warriors led by Opechancanough. All the English colonists were killed, except Smith who was captured and taken several days later to the town of Werowocomoco, the home of Chief Powhatan, about twelve miles from Jamestown. According to Smith, he was welcomed by the chief and offered a feast. Then he was seized and stretched out over two large, flat stones. People loomed over Smith with clubs, when Powhatan gave the word to kill him. Suddenly, Pocahontas rushed forward and held Smith's "head in her arms and laid her owne upon his to save him from death." The girl then helped him to his feet.

Chief Powhatan declared that he and Smith were now allies, and he adopted the Jamestown leader as his son—as a chief subordinate to himself. It is now believed that this incident was actually a mock execution and rescue ceremony, a tradition among the Powhatan in which Pocahontas acted a part in the ritual. In any case, she and Smith did become friends.

In this illustration, Pocahontas makes a dramatic plea to save the life of Captain John Smith.

With his hand on his sword, Captain John Smith, leader of the Jamestown Colony, poses proudly for this formal portrait.

Relations between the Powhatan and the English colonists remained uneasy yet peaceful over the next year. A frequent visitor to Jamestown, Pocahontas brought messages from her father and accompanied people who brought food and furs to trade for hatchets and other goods. When the young men of the colony did cartwheels, "she would follow and wheele some herself, naked as she was all the fort over." During her visits she often chatted with John Smith and probably admired him. Her lively nature and self-assurance made a good impression on the colonists, including Smith. Several years after their first encounter, he described her as "a child of tenne yeares old, which not only for feature, countenance, and proportion much exceedeth any of the rest of his (Powhatan's) people but for wit and spirit (is) the only non-pariel of his countrie."

In October 1609, John Smith was seriously injured in a gunpowder explosion and forced to return to England. After Smith's departure, relations between the Powhatan and the colonists worsened. Trade continued, but tension increased. Once allowed to come and go seemingly as she pleased, Pocahontas now stayed away from the fort at Jamestown. When Pocahontas next visited, she was misinformed that her friend John Smith had died. It is believed that she married a Powhatan "pryvate Captayne" named Kocoum in 1610. Although she lived quietly with her people for a time, she was destined for fame among the English. When Captain Samuel Argall, an ambitious and resourceful member of the Jamestown colony, learned of her whereabouts, he schemed to kidnap her and hold her for ransom. With the help of Japazaws, a lesser chief of the Patawomeck people, Argall tricked Pocahontas into boarding his ship. He told her that she was a prisoner and she "began to be exceeding pensive and discontented," but she eventually became resigned to her captivity.

Argall sent word to Chief Powhatan that he would return his beloved daughter if the chief released several English prisoners held by the Indians, along with property the natives had stolen. After some time Powhatan sent a portion of the ransom and asked that his daughter be treated well. Pocahontas was eventually moved to a new settlement, Henrico, which was governed by Sir Thomas Dale. Here she learned about Christianity and met John Rolfe, a prosperous tobacco planter in July 1613. Allowed to move freely about the settlement, she came to enjoy a role as peacemaker between the colonists and her people. About a year after her capture, Dale led Pocahontas and a force of about 150 men into her father's territory in an attempt to obtain the rest of her ransom. Attacked by the Powhatan, the English retaliated by burning many houses and killing several warriors. Pocahontas was finally released and reunited with two of her brothers. She told them that she had been treated well and that she was in love with John Rolfe. She wanted to marry him.

Powhatan gave his consent and the colonists left, apparently pleased at the prospect of the marriage, although they never received the full ransom. Deeply religious, John Rolfe agonized for several weeks over whether to marry Pocahontas who was a heathen in his eyes. He finally agreed to marry Pocahontas after she converted to Christianity, "for the good of the plantation, the honor of our country, for the glory of God, for mine own salvation." Baptized and christened Rebecca, Pocahontas married John Rolfe on April 5, 1614. The marriage helped to foster peace and goodwill between the English and the Powhatan.

In the spring of 1616 Pocahontas, along with her husband, their young son Thomas, and about a dozen Powhatans, accompanied Sir Thomas Dale on a voyage back to London. Dale sought additional financial support for the Virginia Company, so he brought Pocahontas and the other Powhatan people to attract widespread

Lavishly attired in European dress, Pocahontas, daughter of Chief Powhatan, poses for this early illustration.

public attention to his cause. Greeted as the daughter of an emperor and a princess, Pocahontas was greatly admired. She was presented to King James I, Queen Anne, and the royal family. She also met

Captain John Smith, whom she believed was dead. According to Smith, she was so overcome at seeing him that she at first could not speak with him. After composing herself, Pocahontas talked of their times together, calling him "father." When he objected, she answered, "Were you not afraid to come into my father's Countrie, and caused feare in him and all of his people and feare you here I should call you father: I tell you I will, and you shall call mee childe, and so I will be for ever and ever your Countrieman." She had not seen him for eight years, and as it turned out, this was to be their last meeting.

Seven months later, John Rolfe decided to take his family to Virginia. In March 1617, they set sail, but Pocahontas became ill with an unknown disease, possibly pneumonia or smallpox, and it soon became apparent that she would not survive the long voyage home. She was taken ashore, and, as she lay dying, she comforted her husband by saying, "All must die. 'Tis enough that the child liveth." Just twenty-two years old when she passed away, Pocahontas was buried in the yard at St. George's Parish Church in Gravesend, England.

Pocahontas played a key role in American history—as a real person. As a compassionate girl, she helped the colonists obtain desperately needed food from her people, insuring that Jamestown would not become another "Lost Colony" like Roanoke. In 1616, John Smith wrote that Pocahontas was "the instrument to [preserve] this colonie from death, famine, and utter confusion." She also fostered peace among her people and the colonists arriving on the shores of Virginia.

Powhatan Language

All the Powhatan tribes spoke languages in the Algonquian family—one of the most widespread language families in North America. Tribes in the same language group may have had common ancestors long ago, but they did not necessarily understand each others' language.

Despite attempts to destroy their culture, the Powhatan have demonstrated a strong will to preserve the heritage of their ancestors. Traditions are still honored and vestiges of the language survive in the names of many towns, creeks, rivers, and counties in present-day Virginia.

Here are some words based on *The Dictionary of Powhatan* compiled by William Strachey in the 1600s:

arrowhead	raputtak
ball	aitowh
basket	manote
bear	amonsoquath, momonsacqweo
bird	tshehip, tshetcheindg
boy	vcsapess
bread	apones, appoans
brother	nemat, kemotte
butterfly	manaang-gwas
canoe	aquointan, aquintayne taux
corn parched	rokohamin
crab	tuttascuc

crane	vssac
crow	ohawas
daughter	amonsens
deer	vttapaantam
dog	attemous, attomois
duck	piscoend, pisquaon
eagle	opotenaiok
elder	nussaandg
father	nows, kowse
fire	boketawh, bocuttaw
fish	nammais, namaske, nameche
fox	assimoest, onxe
garden	oronocah
girl	vsqwaseins
goose	kahangoc, kahunge
hatchet	taccahacan, tamahaac, tamohake
hurricane	tohtummocunnum
kettle (copper)	aucutgaqwassan
kettle	aucogwins
knife	damisac, rekasque
leather	uttocais
lightning	kecuttannowas
man	nimatewh
moon	vmpsquoth
muskrat	osasquus
mussel shell	tshecomah

nest (of a bird)	wahchesao
net	aussab, nacowns
otter	pohkevwh, cuttack, rocoyhook
owl	quangatarask
pipe, tobacco	apokan, vppocano
pot	ancagwins
pumpkin	mahcawq
rain	kameyhan, camzowan
reed	nissakan, nehsaakah
river	yocaanta, yeokanta
root	vtchappoc
rushes	cakakesqus
sea	yapam
seeds	amenacacac
shells	ohshaangumiemuns
sister	cursine, nuckaandgum
sky	arrokoth
smoke	kekepemgwah
star	attaanqwassuwk
sun	nepausche, keshowse
turkey	monynawgh, monanaw
turtle	commotins, accomodemsk
village	kaasun
water	suckquohana, secqwahan
wind	rassoum
wood	muskeis

6. New Ways

Today, descendants of the Powhatan Confederacy, including the Mattaponi and the Pamunkey, have their own reservations in Virginia.

IN VIRGINIA TODAY, NATIVE PEOPLE FROM THE POWHATAN CONFEDERACY include the Mattaponi, Rappahannock, Nansemond, Pamunkey, and Chickahominy. Although there are no federally recognized tribes in Virginia, the commonwealth acknowledges eight tribes, including the Mattaponi and the Pamunkey. With their own reservations, these two tribes have lived on the same land, generation after generation, since the seventeenth century. Before World War II, the Mattaponi and Pamunkey supported themselves primarily through farming. Today, reservation lands are divided into farming tracts and hunting territories. The Rappahannock and Chickahominy continue to farm their lands, while others have turned to hunting, trapping, and fishing with gill nets and trotlines, as well as rod and reel. Both the Mattaponi and Pamunkey run state-funded shad fisheries on their reservations. To support themselves, people also make and sell white-oak baskets, pottery, and other hand-crafted goods at shops on the reservations and nearby towns. Many people now commute to jobs in Richmond and other larger cities in Virginia.

The tribes of tidewater Virginia govern themselves. Every four years they elect a chief and council of from four to eight members. The council enforces the written laws of the tribe, which are kept secret from outsiders. Among the Pamunkey, these laws have existed since 1887. The council also manages business affairs relating to reservation lands and chooses trustees from among the local people. These trustees advise and assist the tribe on economic matters. The chief represents the tribe to the outside world. He is chosen for his personal ability—the position is no longer inherited. If the chief does

This woman demonstrates traditional crafts at the Powhatan village at the Jamestown Settlement.

a good job, he will likely be reelected, often for several terms. Among the most highly respected traditional leaders was Chief Black Hawk who served for many years as chief of the Rappanhannock.

Schools have played an important role in maintaining Powhatan culture. At one time, the native peoples of Virginia were not allowed to attend public schools. Children went to school through seventh grade at small private schools of the Chickahominies and Upper Mattaponis or at the reservation school for the Pamunkey and Mattaponi. The Rappahannock and Nansemond had no schools. The

Nansemond though were allowed to attend schools with white students. Most of the teachers in these schools were Native Americans, and students learned about their heritage and traditional arts and crafts. Integration in the 1960s led to the closing of several schools and the busing of children, which parents strongly resented. After their schools closed, people came to rely more heavily on their churches to help them maintain their cultural identity.

Except for the Nansemond, some of whom are Methodist, most of the native peoples in eastern Virginia are Baptists. Many groups have churches of their own. The oldest is the Pamunkey Indian Baptist Church, founded in 1865.

Most of the descendants of the Powhatan tribes now live in Virginia. The Powhatan Renape Nation, however, has a reservation in New Jersey. These people now refer to themselves as Renape, which means "human." Today, the term *Powhatan* more commonly refers to this political organization, while *Renape* reflects their social and cultural heritage as a native people. The nation traces its origins to the late nineteenth century when, one by one, people moved to small communities known as Morrisville and Delair in Pennsauken Township in New Jersey. Most were Rappahannocks from Virginia and Nanticokes from Delaware. Despite prejudice, they proudly maintained their identity as a native people. They married other native people and raised families. Over time, they invited other members, and their community grew. At one time, Powhatan Renape people, living in forty-two homes, made up nearly ninety percent of the population of Morrisville.

In the 1960s, the tribe established a center in Philadelphia, which later relocated to Moorestown, New Jersey. In 1976 the tribe moved to larger quarters in Medford, and in 1980, the state of New Jersey recognized the community as the Powhatan Renape Nation. In 1982, the Powhatan Renape Nation negotiated an agreement with New Jersey to acquire 350 acres of state-owned land in the town of Westampton. The site is now recognized by the state as the Rankokus Indian Reservation. An administrative center there manages educational, cultural, and social programs of the Powhatan Renape Nation.

Tribal members seek to help others understand the history, culture, and traditional way of life of the Powhatan people. Each year, thousands of schoolchildren visit the reservation and its museum, art gallery, exhibits, and nature trails. The tribe also hosts the Juried American Indian Arts Festival (the largest such event east of the Mississippi River) and other annual events.

The Powhatan Confederacy flourished from only about 1570 to 1650, but descendants of the original tribes have survived to this day. Estimates of the total number of people of Powhatan descent vary from 2,000 to 4,000. Most live in Virginia and other East Coast states. Many have distinguished themselves as teachers, artists, and other professionals. Wherever they now make their home, the Powhatan cherish the traditions of those who have gone before them and look forward to a bright future for themselves and their children.

More About

the Powhatan

Time Line

about A.D. 800 Corn is introduced to Virginia.

about 1200 Virginia natives establish permanent towns.

1606 The Virginia Company of England recruits people to establish a colony in America.

1607 105 men and boys land at Jamestown to establish the first permanent English settlement in the New World. Paspahegh Indians attack the colonists, killing two and wounding ten people. Built in a triangular shape, James Fort is completed. John Smith, leader of the colony, is captured by the Powhatan and supposedly saved by Pocahontas in December.

1608 Smith returns from Powhatan's camp. Only 38 of the original 105 colonists have survived the bitter cold.

In their first formal meeting Chief Powhatan receives John Smith and Christopher Newport who have come to trade for provisions.

1609 Injured in a gunpowder blast, John Smith returns to London. Colonists suffer in what becomes known as the "Starving Time."

1610 Jamestown is briefly abandoned, but Lord De La Warre arrives and orders the colonists to return to the settlement.

1613 Pocahontas is brought to Jamestown as a captive.

1614 John Rolfe ships the first Virginia tobacco to England. John Rolfe and Pocahontas are married.

1616 John Rolfe and Pocahontas arrive in London.

1617 Pocahontas dies in Gravesend, England.

1618 Chief Powhatan dies.

1622 Led by Chief Powhatan's brother, Opechancanough, the Powhatan make a surprise attack on the Virginia plantations, massacring 350 people. Jamestown is spared.

1623 Population of Jamestown grows from 400 in 1618 to 4,500 people.

1624 The Virginia Company loses its charter; Virginia becomes a royal province of England.

1631 John Smith dies at the age of 51.

1644 Opechancanough orders a second massacre. Over 500 colonists are killed. Opechancanough is captured and shot in the back by a Jamestown resident.

1651 A reservation is established near present-day Richmond, Virginia, for the Powhatan.

1669 Powhatan population has plunged to 2,900 due to warfare, starvation, and disease.

1676 Queen Anne of the Pamunkey provides warriors to help put down Bacon's Rebellion, an uprising led by Nathaniel Bacon in which rebels burned down Jamestown.

1699 The capital of Virginia is moved from Jamestown to Williamsburg. Jamestown dies as a city.

Virginia passes "An Act to Preserve Racial Integrity," outlawing marriage between different races and denying certain rights to anyone not 100 percent white. However, the law would have included many prominent families, notably the Bollings and Randolphs, who are descendants of John Rolfe and Pocahontas. Legislators then enacted the "Pocahontas Exception" in which peple with one sixteenth Native American blood were considered white. If Pocahontas, who saved the Virginia colony, had married John Rolfe after passage of the law, she would have been sent to prison—in the commonwealth where she is considered "The Mother of Us All."

1980 The state of New Jersey recognizes the Powhatan Renape Nation.

Notable People

Anne (Queen Anne) (died 1725), wife of Totopotomoi, became the leader of the Pamunkey when her husband died. Members of the Powhatan Confederacy, the Pamunkey lived at the fork of the Pamunkey and Mattaponi Rivers. In 1675, William Berkeley, the governor of Virginia, requested her assistance in fighting the rebels led by Nathaniel Bacon. Attired in native dress, Queen Anne came to council and chastised the colonists for their neglect of her people. When she was promised compensation, she agreed to furnish warriors aid in putting down Bacon's Rebellion in 1676. In honor of her aid, she was awarded a silver badge inscribed, "Queen of Pamunkey."

Jack D. Forbes (1934–   ), of Powhatan and Lenape descent, was born in Long Beach, California, and grew up in Southern California. He earned a bachelor's degree (1953), master's degree (1955), and Ph.D (1959) in anthropology from the University of Southern California. In the 1960s he became an activist in the Native American Movement, the Coalition of Eastern Native Americans, and the United Native Americans. He was also a cofounder and instructor at Deganawidah-Quetzalcoatl (D-Q) University. In 1969, he joined the Native American Studies program at the University of California at Davis where he served as a faculty member and department chairperson.

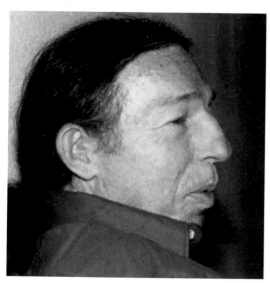

Jack D. Forbes

Forbes has published a number of significant books including *Warriors of the Colorado: the Yumas of Quechan Nation and their Neighbors* (1965), *The Indian in America's Past* (1964), *Native Americans of California and Nevada* (1969), and *Native Americans and Nixon: Presidential Politics and Minority Self-Determination, 1969–1972* (1981).

Namontack (died 1610) became an ally of the colonists at Jamestown. In 1608, Captain Christopher Newport arranged for a young English man, Thomas Savage, to live with the Powhatan to learn their language and customs. In exchange, Chief Powhatan sent Namontack to live with the colonists. Namontack helped the English to obtain urgently needed food and to prevent attacks from hostile warriors. With Newport he journeyed to England where he became familiar with the English language and customs. During the return voyage, he was killed in an argument with a native companion.

Wayne Newton (1942–   ), whose father was half-Powhatan and mother half-Cherokee, was born in Norfolk, Virginia. At the age of six, he began singing on local radio stations, and as a teenager he had his own radio program in Phoenix, Arizona. At age sixteen, he dropped out of school to perform with his brother Jerry. While on the road, Newton met the singer Bobby Darin who helped him secure a recording contract. In 1963, he had his first hit with "Danke Schoen," which was followed by "Red Roses for a Blue Lady." His next hit did not come until the 1970s when he

Wayne Newton

recorded "Daddy, Don't You Walk So Fast." During the 1980s he established himself as one of the most popular and highly paid entertainers in Las Vegas. He has also succeeded as a real estate investor and owns two ranches in Nevada.

Newton has had roles in several movies and television shows as well. In 1982, he held a benefit for Native Americans at the John F. Kennedy Center. In May 1998, he was named entertainer of the year in the first Native American Music Awards program.

Opechancanough (about 1545–1644), a Pamunkey chief, brother of Powhatan, and uncle of Pocahontas, opposed the English colonists during much of his brother's reign as chief of the Powhatan Confederacy. In 1607, he and three hundred warriors ambushed a hunting party led by Captain John Smith, the only colonist who survived the attack. Opechancanough took Smith as a captive to his brother's town on the York River where, according to legend, the captain was spared through the intercession of Pocahontas. After his release in 1608, Smith led an attack on the Pamunkey town and took Opechancanough as a hostage. Opechancanough was then ransomed for food. When Powhatan died in 1618, his brother Opitchapam became chief of the confederacy, though Opechancanough was actually the dominant leader.

As tobacco became popular in Europe, large numbers of settlers arrived to plant fields in Virginia. They tricked the native peoples into signing away huge tracts of land. As trees were chopped down and game driven away, the Powhatan way of life was threatened. On March 22, 1622, Opechancanough led a surprise attack against the colonists. Hundreds of warriors rushed out of the forest and over the tobacco fields. They killed 347 men, women, and children. In retaliation, the English formed a militia and embarked on a campaign of burning the Powhatan houses and crops. As his people were driven farther inland, Opechancanough agreed to peace talks. But upon their arrival he and his warriors were poisoned and attacked. Opechancanough managed to escape, but the war continued. In 1625, Governor Francis Wyatt led a colonial army that defeated a force of more than 1,000 warriors at the town of Uttamussack on the Pamunkey River.

Both sides continued their raids until 1632 when they agreed on a truce. However, twelve years later, on April 18, 1644, Opechancanough called for another attack. Reputedly more than a hundred years old, the chief had to be carried to the site of the battle on a litter. Sweeping through the colony, his warriors killed nearly five hundred men, women, and children out of a total population of nearly eight thousand people. The colonists again retaliated with a military campaign in which Opechancanough was captured and carried back to Jamestown on his litter. Mocked by the colonists, he was later shot by an angry guard.

Upon the death of Opechancanough, his successor, Necotowance, surrendered all Powhatan legal rights to their ancestral land, and the Powhatan Confederacy vanished as a political and military entity in Virginia.

Pocahontas (about 1595–1617) was a favorite daughter of Chief Powhatan. According to legend, in 1608, when she was about thirteen years old, Pocahontas intervened to save the life of Captain John Smith, the leader of Jamestown, who had been captured by her uncle Opechancanough. When her father was about to club Captain Smith to death, she supposedly asked that his life be spared. However, in his later published account, Smith did not mention her having any role in the incident.

After Smith left for England in 1609, relations worsened between the natives and the colonists. In 1612, Pocahontas was lured onto an English ship on the Potomac River and taken to Jamestown as a captive. The colonists hoped to exchange her for prisoners held by Chief Powhatan. While at Jamestown, Pocahontas converted to Christianity. She was also courted by John Rolfe and, with her father's permission, married him in April 1613. Her marriage helped to insure peaceful relations between the colonists and the Powhatan.

In 1616, Pocahontas sailed to England with her husband and several other Powhatan, including her brother-in-law Uttamatomac. Welcomed as

Pocahontas

a princess and the daughter of an emperor, she met King James I and Queen Anne, the rulers of England. Her portrait was painted, and she met John Smith again. In 1617, as she prepared to return to America, Pocahontas died of an unknown disease at Gravesend, England. She was buried in the yard at St. George's Church, where a memorial to her is in place. The following year her father died, and in 1622 her husband, John Rolfe, was killed when her uncle Opechancanough went to war against the colonists.

Pocahontas had a son, Thomas Rolfe, who was educated in London. He returned to Virginia in 1641 and became a prosperous businessman. However, because of conflicts between the colonists and native peoples, he had to petition Virginia authorities to visit his Powhatan relatives. Several Virginia families have traced their ancestry through Thomas Rolfe to Pocahontas and Chief Powhatan.

Powhatan (Wahunsonacock, Wahunsenacawh) (about 1547–1618) was chief of the Powhatan Confederacy founded by his father. He was known as Powhatan among the English colonists at Jamestown. Powhatan expanded and strengthened the alliance into about thirty tribes living in the Tidewater region. His principal town was Werowocomoco on the north bank of the York River. Powhatan had many wives and children, including a favorite daughter named Pocahontas.

During a period of tense peace with the colonists at Jamestown, Powhatan and other leaders, including Namontack, provided the colonists with food and taught them how to plant corn. Powhatan's daughter helped to maintain peaceful relations, especially after she married John Rolfe, an English colonist. Powhatan and Captain John Smith, the leader of Jamestown, cautiously respected each other. Smith apparently declared Powhatan to be "king" of the region as a way of appeasing the leader.

Around 1610, Powhatan moved farther west to Orapax between the Chickahominy and Pamunkey Rivers to get away from the colonists who were arriving in greater numbers in Virginia.

Totopotomoi (died 1656), a chief of the Pamumkey tribe, maintained peaceful relations with colonists in Virginia after the death of Opechancanough in 1644. He provided nearly a hundred warriors to a force of about the same number of colonists in 1656. Led by Colonel Edward Hill, this militia sought to repel inland tribes which had moved into territory near the falls of the James River where Totopotomoi's people had once lived. At a peace meeting, Hill ordered his men to seize and execute five chiefs of the enemy. In the fierce battle that ensued, Totopotomoi and most of his warriors were killed. Hill was later found guilty of improper conduct and suspended from military service, but he remained prominently involved in Virginia politics. Totopotomoi's wife, Anne, assumed leadership of the Pamunkey.

Glossary

Algonquian Most widespread group, or family, of languages spoken throughout North America. Many Native Americans tribes speak Algonquian, including the Arapaho, Cheyenne, Blackfoot, Fox, Shawnee, Abenaki, and Delaware, and the Powhatan tribes.

breechcloth A cloth or skin worn between the legs; also breechclout.

buckskin Deer hide softened by tanning or curing.

confederacy An alliance or union of groups. Many Virginia tribes formed a confederacy under Chief Powhatan.

dugout A type of canoe made by hollowing out a tree trunk.

huskanaw A special coming-of-age ceremony in which selected young men underwent a rigorous initiation.

kwiocos Priest of the tribes in the Powhatan Confederacy who led religious ceremonies and advised on political matters.

lacrosse A modern sport based upon a popular stickball game of Native Americans living in the forests of eastern North America.

mamanatowick The principal leader of the Powhatan Confederacy.

moccasins Soft leather shoes often decorated with brightly colored beads.

Okeus Principal god of the Powhatan.

Powhatan A term referring to a small Virginia tribe, a confederacy of tribes in Virginia, or their leader, Chief Powhatan.

sweat lodge A heated, dome-shaped hut covered with bark or mats in which men and women purify themselves for ritual purposes.

Tidewater Coastal lowlands around Chesapeake Bay and along the Atlantic coast in present-day Virginia and Maryland.

treaty A signed, legal agreement between two nations.

tribute Payment made by subjects to their ruler.

weir A wooden fence or row of rocks built in a stream to trap fish or force them into a narrow channel where they can be easily netted or speared.

weroance A chief or leader of a Powhatan tribe. Also *werowance*. Female leaders were known as *weronsqua*.

wigwam A domed house made of a bent branch frame covered with sheets of bark or woven mats.

Further Information

Readings

Many excellent books have been published about the Powhatan tribes, including the observations of early visitors, such as Thomas Hariot who published *A Briefe and True Report of the New Found Land of Virginia*, in 1588, and William Strachey who published *The Historie of Travell into Virginia Britania (1612)*. The retelling of "The Creation Story" is based upon a description in Strachey's book.

The following books, many of which were consulted when writing this book, are recommended for anyone who would like to learn more about the Powhatan:

Axtell, James. *The Rise and Fall of the Powhatan Empire: Indians in Seventeenth-Century Virginia*. Williamsburg, VA: Colonial Williamsburg Foundation, 1995.

Barbour, Philip L. *Pocahontas and Her World: A Chronicle of America's First Settlement in Which Is Related the Story of the Indians and the Englishmen, Particularly Captain John Smith, Captain Samuel Argall, and Master John Rolfe*. Boston: Houghton Mifflin, 1970.

Crazy Horse, Roy. *A Brief History of the Powhatan-Renape Nation*. Rancocas, NJ: Powhatan Renape Nation, 1986.

Gleach, Frederic W. *Powhatan's World and Colonial Virginia: A Conflict of Cultures*. Lincoln: University of Nebraska Press, 1997.

Lemay, J. A. Leo. *Did Pocahontas Save Captain John Smith?* Athens: University of Georgia Press, 1992.

McCary, Ben C. *Indians in Seventeenth Century Virginia*. Baltimore: Genealogical Pub. Co., 1995.

Mossiker, Frances. *Pocahontas: The Life and the Legend*. New York: Knopf, 1976.

Rasmussen, William M. S. *Pocahontas: Her Life & Legend*. Richmond: Virginia Historical Society, 1994.

Rountree, Helen C. *Pocahontas's People: The Powhatan Indians of Virginia through Four Centuries*. Norman: University of Oklahoma Press, 1996.

————. *Powhatan Foreign Relations, 1500–1722*. Charlottesville: University Press of Virginia, 1993.

————. *The Powhatan Indians of Virginia: Their Traditional Culture*. Norman: University of Oklahoma Press, 1989.

Speck, Frank Gouldsmith. *Chapters on Ethnology of the Powhatan Tribes of Virginia*. New York: Museum of the American Indian, Heye Foundation, 1928.

Strachey, William. *A Dictionary of Powhatan*. Southampton, PA: Evolution Pub., 1999.

Woodward, Grace Steele. *Pocahontas*. Norman: University of Oklahoma Press, 1969.

Children's Books

Here are some children's books about the Powhatan, including books about Pocahontas. Although these are fictionalized accounts of her life, they may be of interest and value in learning about the Powhatan.

Covert, Kim. *The Powhatan People*. Mankato, MN: Bridgestone Books, 1999.

Feest, Christian F. *The Powhatan Tribes*. New York: Chelsea House, 1990.

Fritz, Jean. *The Double Life of Pocahontas*. New York: Putnam, 1983.

Holler, Anne. *Pocahontas: Powhatan Peacemaker*. New York: Chelsea House, 1993.

Iannone, Catherine. *Pocahontas*. New York: Chelsea House, 1995.

Lund, Bill, and Covert, Kim. *Powhatan People*. Children's Press, 1998.

McDaniel, Melissa. *The Powhatan Indians*. New York: Chelsea House, 1995.

Penner, Lucille Recht. *The True Story of Pocahontas*. New York: Random House, 1994.

Raphael, Elaine. *Pocahontas: Princess of the River Tribes*. New York: Scholastic, 1993.

Wilkie, Katharine Elliott. *Pocahontas, Indian Princess*. Champaign, IL: Garrard Publishing Co., 1969.

Organizations

Jamestown-Yorktown Foundation
P.O. Box 1607
Williamsburg, VA 23187-1607
(757) 253-4838
Fax: (757) 253-5299

Mattaponi Indian Reservation
RFD 1, P.O. Box 667
West Point, VA 23181
(804) 769-4508

Pamunkey Indian Reservation
Rt. 1, Box 2220
King William, VA 23086
(804) 843-4740

Powhatan Renape Nation
Rankokus Indian Reservation
P.O. Box 225
Rancocas, NJ 08073
(609) 261-4747
Fax: (609) 261-7313

Websites

Several of the following websites were consulted while researching and writing this book. These sites may be helpful to you in learning more about the Powhatan.

Jamestown
http://www.williamsburg.com/james/james.html

Jamestown Historic Briefs

http://www.nps.gov/colo/Jthanout/JTBriefs.html

Jamestown 1607–1630

http://ab.mec.edu/jamestown/jamestown.html

The Real Pocahontas

http://www.geocities.com/Broadway/1001/poca.html

Jamestowne Society: Pocahontas

http://www.jamestowne.org/History4.htm

Powhatan History

http://www.powhatan.org/history.html

Rankokus Indian Reservation

http://www.powhatan.org/

Virginia Archeology Links

http://geog.gmu.edu/gess/classes/geog380/6_links.html

Virginia Indians : The Powhatan : Index

http://falcon.jmu.edu/~ramseyil/vaindianspowindex.htm

Virginia's Indian Tribes: The Powhatan Confederacy

http://falcon.jmu.edu/~ramseyil/vaindianspowhatan.htm

Virtual Jamestown

http://jefferson.village.virginia.edu/vcdh/jamestown/

Index

Raymond Bial

HAS PUBLISHED MORE THAN THIRTY CRITICALLY ACCLAIMED BOOKS OF PHOtographs for children and adults. His photo-essays for children include *Corn Belt Harvest, Amish Home, Frontier Home, Shaker Home, The Underground Railroad, Portrait of a Farm Family, With Needle and Thread: A Book About Quilts, Mist Over the Mountains: Appalachia and Its People, Cajun Home,* and *Where Lincoln Walked.*

He is currently immersed in writing *Lifeways,* a series of books about Native Americans. As with his other work, Bial's deep feeling for his subjects is evident in both the text and illustrations. He travels to tribal cultural centers, photographing homes, artifacts, and surroundings and learning firsthand about the national lifeways of these peoples.

A full-time library director at a small college in Champaign, Illinois, he lives with his wife and three children in nearby Urbana.